KT-457-664

Food supplies often ran low. In 1670, Henry Morgan's crew of pirates had to eat roasted leather satchels!

POPULATION: ONE!

There were tough punishments for pirates who broke their ship's code. If they stole from another crew member or tried to desert from the ship, they could end up marooned on a island. All they would be left wit was some water and pistol, so the chance surviving was slim.

Lime

Captain Keitt

SCURVY KNAVES

A pirate's diet was not a healthy one. Meat was dried and salted and hard work to gnaw through! Drinking water was in short supply and the lack of vitamin C obtained from fresh fruit and vegetables caused many pirates to suffer from a disease called scurvy, which could be fatal.

PIRATES QUIZ

What was 'hard tack'?

a) a biscuit
b) a punishment
c) a part of the sail

What was the common punishment for a pirate who hit a crew member?

a) no food for three days
b) 40 lashes on the bare back
c) a day tied to the mast

Which Scottish sailor spent four years marooned on a desert island?

a) Steven Cameron
b) James McDonald
c) Alexander Selkirk

(answers on page 32)

3

WARRIOR WOMEN

Most ships only allowed men on board. So for many women who wanted to sail the high seas, the only answer was to dress and act like men!

PIRATES QUIZ

What was Alwilda's husband called?

a) Alf
b) Ralph
c) Olaf

How many pirates did Ching Shih command?

a) 8,000
b) 18,000
c) 80,000

Which actress played a pirate in *Cutthroat Island*?

a) Sandra Bullock
b) Geena Davis
c) Julia Roberts

(answers on page 32)

BONNY ON BOARD

Anne Bonny became a pirate after meeting Captain Jack Rackham. Together, the pair terrorised Spanish treasure ships until they were captured in 1720. Rackham was hanged but Anne escaped the death penalty because she was pregnant.

Anne Bonny

READ ON!

Mary Read disguised herself as a man to join Jack Rackham's pirate crew. As the picture shows, her victims were amazed when they discovered she was a woman. Read was a fearless fighter – only she and Anne Bonny fought back when Rackham's ship was captured by the British navy!

BLOODTHIRSTY PIRATES

by **Richard Mead**

Contents

Clever Clogs Books

Copyright © 2006 ticktock Entertainment Ltd.
http://www.ticktock.co.uk

501 081 907

THIEVES ABOARD!

Bold, adventurous, and often bloodthirsty, pirates terrorised the seas for thousands of years. These ocean-going robbers plundered ships for treasure, hoping for great rewards. But life as a pirate was never easy...

TREASURE ISLAND

In the sixteenth century, major trade routes opened up between Europe and the Far East. Ships laden with gold and silver sailed the Indian Ocean, offering rich pickings for pirates. The island of Madagascar, situated off the east coast of Africa, became a pirate kingdom as it was an ideal base for hunting out passing trade ships. So great were the rewards that, at one time, the island attracted around 1,500 pirates!

KEEPING THE CODE

Life at sea offered certain freedoms, but pirates couldn't always do whatever they wanted. Most ships had their own code of conduct which the crew had to obey.

The code often included rules about gambling and also banned women from going aboard the boat!

FOOD FOR THOUGHT

A Scandinavian princess called Alwilda is supposed to have became a pirate to avoid marrying a Danish prince. When the prince was sent to bring her back, she was so impressed by his fighting skills that she agreed!

BERRY FIERCE!

Charlotte De Berry joined the British navy, pretending to be a man. When she was attacked by her captain, she led a mutiny against him and cut off his head. Charlotte took command and the crew became pirates.

SHIH'S IN CHARGE

In the nineteenth century, a woman called Ching Shih inherited a huge pirate empire from her husband. At one point, she controlled a fleet of 1,800 boats which terrorised the coast of China. When Ching Shih surrendered, thousands of her men swapped sides and joined the navy.

Mary Read

PIRATES QUIZ

The Greeks used triremes against pirates. What were these?

a) catapults
b) spears
c) warships

Which of these was a famous Viking pirate?

a) Sweyn Forkbeard
b) Gunthar Knifenose
c) Harald Spoonface

What does the word 'viking' mean?

a) to sail quickly
b) to go on a sea raid
c) to destroy by fire

(answers on page 32)

PREMIER PIRATES

Piracy has a long history – it even features in ancient Greek art and writing. In the first century BC, pirates were a menace to Roman trade. Hundreds of years later, in northern Europe, Viking warriors plundered the seas.

SEA CHANGE

In one ancient Greek myth, the god of wine, Dionysus was captured by pirates. The angry god transformed himself into a lion and his frightened captors hurled themselves into the sea, where they were turned into dolphins!

RANSOMED ROMAN

Julius Caesar

Before he became Roman Emperor, Julius Caesar was captured by pirates. In 78 BC, he was held hostage on a tiny island for over six weeks until the ransom had been paid. After he was released, he returned with a group of soldiers and killed all of his kidnappers.

TOAST THE COAST

More than a thousand years ago, Viking pirates began to attack parts of northern Europe. They brought terror to coastal towns, torching houses and pillaging for treasure and slaves. Churches and abbeys were prime targets, as they often contained many valuable items.

Scene from The Vikings film, 1958

SIZE SURPRISE!

A pirate once told the ruler of Greece, Alexander the Great (356-323 BC), that they both troubled the world. 'Because I do it in a small ship, I am called a pirate,' he said. 'When you do it with a great fleet, you are called an emperor!'

LONG JOURNEYS

The Vikings were fearsome warriors who designed their ships for war. They sailed in longships made from oak, which could carry up to 50 men. The boats had a single sail on a pine mast and were very fast. The Vikings used oars to row the longships swiftly to the shore.

LEAGUE LEADERS

In the Middle Ages, pirates tormented shipping on the Baltic Sea in Northern Europe. Some German merchants, who were suffering heavy losses, banded together and designed a new ship called a cog. With a fortified bow and stern and high sides, it was a difficult vessel to board!

Cog ship

PIRATES QUIZ

How many cannons did Spanish galleons usually carry?

a) 12
b) 30
c) 60

What is a rudder used for?

a) hoisting the sail
b) pumping out sea water
c) steering the ship

Which fifteenth-century English ship had high fighting decks at each end?

a) the nef
b) the jef
c) the ref

(answers on page 32)

STRENGTH IN NUMBERS

In the sixteenth century, Spanish galleons were used to carry treasure to Europe from North and South America. But these heavy ships weren't good in battle and were easy pickings for pirates. To protect their booty, galleons travelled in convoys of up to 100 ships.

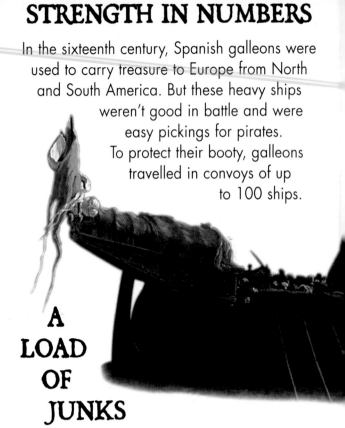

A LOAD OF JUNKS

Pirate junks were a scary sight in the Far East. They were captured cargo ships, which the pirates adapted for attacking other boats. The largest junks were around 30 metres long, and could carry up to 400 men. Serious fire-power was added, too – there was room for 30 cannons!

SHIP SHAPE

Some pirates built their attack ships, but many simply stole ships from their enemies. Meanwhile, their unlucky victims had to find ways to defend themselves from these bloodthirsty sea-robbers.

Barbary pirates

THE RAM RAMP

In the seventeenth century, Muslim pirates called corsairs used galleys to chase after their victims. A galley had a battering ram at the front for smashing into the sides of enemy boats. When the two ships were close, the ram would be used as a bridge for boarding the enemies boat.

BARNACLE BUILD-UP

Pirates had to be good with a bucket and mop! The hulls needed cleaning every few months to stop barnacles and seaweed slowing the ship down.

PIRATE POSSESSIONS

Pirates had a job to do, for which they had their own 'tools of the trade'. As well as weapons for fighting, they needed tools for building and looking after their ships, and of course, clothes to carry out such tasks!

FANCY DRESS?

Real pirates didn't look like the ones we see in the movies. Their clothes were tattered and they never washed – the only time they got wet was when when they jumped into the sea! They certainly wouldn't have kept a parrot as a pet – they'd probably have eaten it instead!

PIRATES QUIZ

What is a dirk?

a) an axe
b) a dagger
c) a gun

Which of these is part of a pistol's firing mechanism?

a) frizzen
b) blixen
c) quassle

Why was brass used to make guns?

a) it was very cheap
b) it doesn't rust
c) it's very light

(answers on page 32)

10

TOOL TIME

Boat-building was a complicated process. An axe called an adze was used to turn tree trunks into planks. The gaps or seams between the planks were filled with rope fibres then sealed with tar to stop the water getting in. After the boat was put to sea, regular repairs were necessary, using a tool called a caulking iron.

Long John Silver

FIGHTING FUND

Pirates injured in battle usually received compensation from the captain. Losing a finger was worth about 100 pieces of silver, while a leg could be worth eight times as much.

SECOND-HAND

Weapons used by pirates were often stolen from their victims. In the seventeenth century, the cutlass, with its short blade, was very popular. Daggers could be hidden in clothes for surprise attacks. Pirates also swung sharpened iron discs on cords – another effective weapon against enemies!

PISTOL PROBLEMS

Guns were popular weapons with pirates – from long-range muskets to smaller pistols. But they weren't always useful. When the sea was choppy, aiming guns accurately could be difficult. As reloading took a long time, pirates often used a gun's butt to bash enemies over the head!

Antique pistol

PIRATES QUIZ

When is the earliest record of the name 'Jolly Roger' being used?

a) 1699
b) 1724
c) 1741

Black and white pirate flags became known as...

a) blackjollies
b) jollyjacks
c) blackjacks

Why did some Chinese pirates put bats on their flags?

a) to bring good luck
b) to frighten other sailors
c) to scare birds away from food supplies

(answers on page 32)

HAVE A HEART

Blackbeard was one of the most terrifying pirates of all time. His flag showed the figure of a skeleton. In one hand, this figure is aiming an arrow at a bleeding heart. In the other, it is holding an hourglass. Sailors knew their time had run out when they saw this symbol!

CHEERS!

English-born Bartholomew Roberts became a pirate in around 1720. His Jolly Roger featured himself and the figure of death raising a drink. But after the governors of two Caribbean islands tried to capture him, he flew a new flag. This showed him with the skulls of inhabitants from the two islands!

FRIEND OR FOE?

Pirates sometimes misled enemy ships by flying a 'friendly' flag or even dressing up as women! As the pirates drew close, they would suddenly raise the Jolly Roger just before they started the attack!

FLAG DAY

In the past, spotting an unfamiliar ship approaching would have made any sailor nervous. But if a ship was flying a Jolly Roger, it meant that trouble was certain!

Christopher Moody's flag

RED ALERT

The earliest pirate flags were plain red – the colour of blood! They sent a chilling signal to other crews; no mercy would be given to enemies. This was a sure way to put the wind up most sailors, however brave!

Jack Rackham's flag

Thomas Tew's flag

Henry Avery's flag

SKULL-DUGGERY

Pirate captains often included the skull and crossbones on their flags as a symbol of death. These designs were usually white on a black background, but not always; Christopher Moody (1694-1722) used a red background for his flag.

PIRATES QUIZ

How were the two privateers Francis Drake and John Hawkins related? Were they...
a) brothers-in-law
b) cousins
c) uncle and nephew

Which city did privateer Jean Lafitte help to defend?
a) Boston
b) New Orleans
c) Philadelphia

In 1603, which English king cancelled letters of marque ?
a) Charles I
b) Henry VIII
c) James I

(answers on page 32)

LEGAL THEFT

Privateers were pirates who worked for a government. If a country was at war with another, it would license a ship-owner to attack the enemy's vessels in return for a share of the booty!

WALTER'S WOE

Walter Raleigh was an English adventurer who supported privateering. He wanted to use the profits to fund a new colony in North America. Unfortunately, his plans were cut short after a voyage to find gold for King James I (1566-1625). When Raleigh returned empty-handed, the king had him beheaded.

GALLEON GOLD

Francis Drake isn't only famous for sailing around the world and fighting the Armada; he was also a privateer. Drake stole treasure worth more than £100,000 from one Spanish galleon, which he presented to Queen Elizabeth I. It's no wonder she called him 'my pirate'!

Spanish treasure

FRENCH FORTUNE

French privateers made such a fortune plundering English ships that the King of France, Louis XIV (1638-1715) asked if they could lend him some money!

MARQUE MY WORDS

Licences given to privateers were called 'letters of marque'. These documents were also handed out in peacetime. They allowed sailors robbed at sea to attack ships from the pirates' home country – and not be charged with piracy themselves.

TRADE WAR

Born in Scotland, privateer John Paul Jones became an American hero during the War of Independence (1775-83). He attacked British ships, weakening Britain's trade with America. Jones certainly got around – he later joined the Russian navy!

John Paul Jones

PIRATES QUIZ

What were doubloons?

a) gold coins
b) rubies
c) silk trousers

How did the Spanish coins, pieces of eight, get their name?

a) they had eight sides
b) they were worth eight reals
c) only eight were ever made

On which island did William Kidd bury a treasure chest?

a) Easter Island
b) Gardiner's Island
c) Isle of Man

(answers on page 32)

A ROBBER ROBBED?

A famous haul was made by the pirate Henry Avery in 1695. He captured the Mogul ship, the *Gang-i-Sawai*, which was carrying treasure worth £325,000.

Avery then retired, although one story claims he was robbed of all his money by merchants who knew he couldn't report them!

Treasure chest

Spices

SPICE BOYS

Pirates weren't just after money and jewels. Tobacco, sugar and some spices were valuable hauls and could be traded when the crew reached land. Food and drink were also gratefully received if supplies were low.

BURIED BOOTY

Why did people become pirates? To make their fortunes, of course! One pirate became so wealthy he even had a golden mast made for his ship.

ONE FOR YOU...

The pirates' code ruled that all treasure must be shared out among the crew. However, the captain and his officers usually received a bigger share. And some captains tried to get a lot more by sailing off before the plunder had been divided.

TEW MUCH?

In 1693, the American pirate Thomas Tew overpowered a ship returning to Bombay. The vessel was packed with booty and each member of Tew's crew received a share worth £3,000. Today, that share would have been worth over a million pounds.

It's said that Blackbeard once left one of his 14 wives to guard a treasure chest on a desert island. Neither she nor the treasure was ever seen again!

MISSING MONEY

PIRATES QUIZ

What was Blackbeard's real name?

a) James Learned
b) Steven Masters
c) Edward Teach

What did Henry Avery rename his first ship?

a) *The Fancy*
b) *The Fighter*
c) *The Freedom*

What was the pirate Black Bart's favourite drink?

a) rum
b) sea water
c) tea

(answers on page 32)

MORGAN'S MISSIONS

Around 1630, pirates called buccaneers began preying on the Spanish in the Caribbean. The greatest buccaneer ever was Welshman Henry Morgan. He led many daring raids on Spanish ships and colonies, returning after one voyage with 100,000 pieces of eight. King Charles II was so impressed that he made Morgan Deputy Governor of Jamaica.

THE SLIPPERY SLOPE...

William Kidd started off as a successful New York businessman. Then on one voyage, he killed a member of his crew and turned to piracy. Legend claims that he buried his Bible to show he was turning to crime!

Henry Avery

THE ARCH WAY

Henry Avery was so famous he was known as the Arch-Pirate. Part of a privateering expedition, he convinced the crew to mutiny and became their captain. Within a year he was a rich man and had a fleet of six ships!

SUPERIOR SEA-DOGS

What makes a pirate famous? The number of years he spent at sea? The amount of treasure he captured? Or perhaps it's how much he terrified people...

William Kidd

WARNING SHOT

From 1716-18, Blackbeard terrorised the waters off the North American coast. He didn't just scare sailors, he had his own crew cowering, too. He shot his first mate, Israel Hands, claiming that if he didn't kill one of his crew now and then, they would forget who he was!

WHAT A BLAST!

To avoid capture, a pirate called Rahmah bin Jabr set light to the gunpowder store on his ship. He blew himself up but also destroyed half of the attacking ships!

GOING GLOBAL

From the Caribbean to the South China Seas, sailors were rarely safe from pirates. Although names and customs differed from place to place, there was always someone ready to attack...

Dao sword

HAIR TODAY...

Before he became a pirate, Chui Apoo worked as a barber in Hong Kong!

RED DREAD

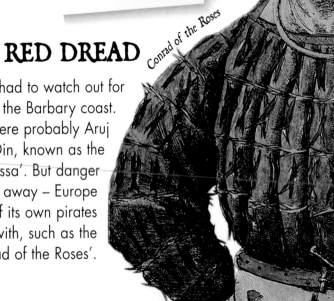

Conrad of the Roses

European ships had to watch out for Muslim corsairs on the Barbary coast. The most famous were probably Aruj and Kheir-ed-Din, known as the 'Brothers Barbarossa'. But danger wasn't always so far away – Europe had plenty of its own pirates to contend with, such as the German, 'Conrad of the Roses'.

FIERCE FLEET

This is a *dao* sword, which is decorated with tufts of human hair. It was a popular weapon with pirates in Southeast Asia. One of the most feared of these was Chui Apoo, who commanded over 500 vessels. But in 1849, his fleet was destroyed by British warships and, after being betrayed by his followers, he died in prison.

FIGHTING FARMERS

The Caribbean was home to the bloodthirsty buccaneers. Many were farmers whose land had been taken by the Spanish, and they were joined by runaway slaves and escaped convicts. Buccaneers often dressed in animal hide and were known to pong a bit!

RAIDING ROVERS

Trade between Europe and the East meant that many boats had to pass through the Indian Ocean. The shipments of jewels, spices and ivory encouraged pirates like the Gujarati Rovers, who spread out their boats 10 km apart, making them difficult for trading ships to avoid.

PIRATES QUIZ

Where is the Barbary coast?

a) North Africa
b) Russia
c) South America

Which buccaneer once spit-roasted two farmers alive?

a) Francis L'Ollonais
b) Henry Morgan
c) Rock Braziliano

Where were the Barbarossa brothers born?

a) Greece
b) Morocco
c) Turkey

(answers on page 32)

PIRATES QUIZ

For what purpose did pirates use a grappling iron?

a) to load a cannon
b) to pull two ships together
c) to attach the sail to the mast

Which musical instrument did Francis Drake take on his voyages?

a) a drum
b) a flute
c) a violin

What were caltrops used for?

a) sharpening cutlasses
b) shouting to another ship
c) spiking the feet of enemies

(answers on page 32)

IT'S A BREEZE!

Treasure ships were often attacked at the beginning of a voyage. That's because they couldn't work up much speed until they found a strong wind to power the sails. Ships leaving the Caribbean would always head north to get a good wind, so crafty pirates would lie in wait off the American coast.

FIRE AWAY

The buccaneer Henry Morgan once found his route blocked by three Spanish warships. As a solution, he got his crew to fit a 'fire ship' with fake guns and wooden sailors. It was launched towards the Spanish boats and burst into flames. Morgan escaped and even captured one of the Spanish ships!

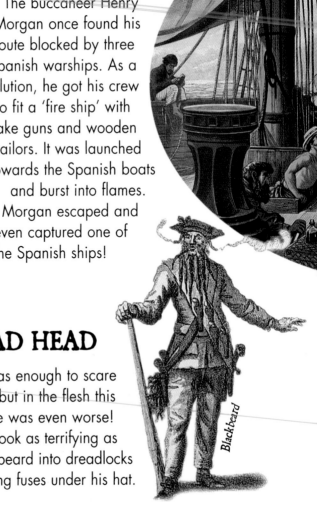

Blackbeard

DREAD HEAD

Blackbeard's name was enough to scare the wits out of sailors, but in the flesh this fearsome pirate was even worse! He made himself look as terrifying as possible by plaiting his beard into dreadlocks and tying smoking fuses under his hat.

TACTIC TIME

Pirates would quite often avoid a fight if they could. But if they did go into battle, they had plenty of clever tactics to give them the upper hand!

WHAT A DIN!

Pirates didn't just use musical instruments for entertainment. When played together, drums and wind instruments could make a real racket. This noise was a useful scare tactic when attacking treasure ships. Pirates added to the chaos by waving their cutlasses and shouting threats – enough to unnerve any enemy!

Pirates pretending to be harmless passengers

Privateer Jonathan Haraden once attacked a ship by standing next to a cannon, holding a burning candle. The ship surrendered, not knowing Jonathan had only one cannon ball!

SINGLE SHOT

PIRATE PUNISHMENTS

PIRATES QUIZ

Why did it take two attempts to hang William Kidd?

a) his crew-mates attempted a rescue
b) the first rope broke
c) the crowd knocked the gallows over

Which punishment involved being dragged through the water?

a) keel-hauling
b) shark-baiting
c) wave-flogging

When was the last pirate executed in Britain?

a) 1785
b) 1840
c) 1903

(answers on page 32)

Being a pirate had its drawbacks. If you weren't killed in battle, there was always the chance you would be caught and executed. Even your own crew-mates could punish you!

Pirate punishment

KNOT NICE

The cat of nine tails was a common punishment at sea. It was a whip made from nine cords of rope, each of which ended in a knot. To add to the torture, the sailor about to be whipped often had to make the cat of nine tails himself.

NO KIDDING!

Dead pirates were often hung in iron cages from a wooden frame called a gibbet. When William Kidd was executed in 1701, his corpse was covered in tar to stop decay and placed at the mouth of the River Thames. It warned other sailors not to become pirates!

Before being executed, a pirate was measured to make sure the gibbet cage was a perfect fit.

KILLING TIME

A pirate sentenced to death on board a ship faced several methods of execution. One was being made to 'walk the plank' into the sea, but this was rare. Usually, condemned pirates were shot, or hurled from high up in the rigging onto the deck.

Walking the plank

LOCKED UP

Privateers who were caught would often end up in prison – usually for good! Prisons were badly overcrowded and disease was common. Often, the only hope was to bribe a guard for food or better conditions.

THE PIRATE POLICE

Governments couldn't just stand by and watch their ships being robbed, so they hired sailors to capture pirates – usually dead or alive!

PIRATES QUIZ

Which pirate was once a pirate hunter?

a) Henry Avery
b) John Rackham
c) William Kidd

What was the reward for capturing the pirate Blackbeard?

a) £10
b) £100
c) £1,000

Why did William James first become a sailor?

a) to avoid a punishment for poaching
b) to sail with his grandfather
c) he was press-ganged

(answers on page 32)

JAMES' AIMS

The Maratha pirates controlled the sea off the west coast of India in the early eighteenth century – until William James came along. In his 40-gun ship, *The Protector*, James sailed close to the Maratha pirates' fort. He bombarded it for two days before it blew up.

The Swallow

HARD TO SWALLOW

The man-of-war was a heavily-armed warship used by the British navy against pirates. One of these ships, *The Swallow*, helped to defeat Bartholomew Roberts ('Black Bart'), off the coast of West Africa. Roberts fought back but was killed by a shot in the neck.

BOAT BOMB

In 1693, the English navy tried to destroy a pirate base using a boat filled with gunpowder. Unfortunately, the boat hit a rock and so the only victim was an unlucky cat!

MAYNARD'S MISSION

Lieutenant Robert Maynard had a tricky job – he was hired to hunt down Blackbeard! Maynard tracked down the famous pirate and fought him on the deck of his ship. Legend has it that Blackbeard received twenty cutlass wounds and five pistol shots before he died.

Duel: Blackbeard vs. Maynard

FOREIGN HUNTER

Singapore came under attack from piracy in the nineteenth century. To stamp out the problem, a £20 reward was offered for the death or capture of each pirate. Captain Farquhar of *HMS Albatross* helped to sink 88 pirate boats – and earned a huge £20,700.

FICTIONAL FIGHTERS

Hook (Dustin Hoffman)

Real or fictional, stories of pirates never fail to entertain us. Today there are numerous books, plays and films telling tall tales about exciting adventures on the high seas.

YOU'RE HOOKED

One of the most famous fictional characters is Captain Hook from the play *Peter Pan*, first staged in 1904. Created by the writer J.M. Barrie, Hook is Peter Pan's enemy and comes to a sticky end when he is eaten by a crocodile. The play eventually became a book, a Disney animation and has inspired several films.

The Sea Hawk (Errol Flynn)

PIRATE POETRY

Lord Byron wrote a famous poem about a pirate in 1814. It was called 'The Corsair', and has since been turned into several operas and even a ballet.

CARTOON CAPERS

Pirates aren't just popular in the movies – they have taken over the small screen, too. Captain Pugwash was created as a comic-strip character in 1950 and went on to become a huge television star. He wasn't very brave, especially when he came face-to-face with Cutthroat Jake!

AAAH, JIM LAD!

In the book *Treasure Island*, cabin-boy Jim Hawkins sails on the *Hispaniola* on a treasure quest, only to discover that half the crew are pirates. Author Robert Louis Stevenson based their leader, Long John Silver, on a friend who only had one leg.

FANTASTIC FLYNN

Errol Flynn was the silver screen's supreme swashbuckler. He became a star after playing a pirate in the film *Captain Blood* (1935). Famed for performing all his own stunts, Flynn also made a big splash in the 1940 film *The Sea Hawk*.

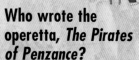

PIRATES QUIZ

Who wrote the operetta, *The Pirates of Penzance*?

a) Bernstein and Sondheim
b) Gilbert and Sullivan
c) Lennon and McCartney

What is the name of Captain Pugwash's ship?

a) *The Black Pig*
b) *The Grey Ghost*
c) *The White Whale*

Who is the retired pirate in *Swallows and Amazon*?

a) Captain Flint
b) Captain Match
c) Captain Spark

(answers on page 32)

PIRATES QUIZ

What was Lai Choi San's nickname?

a) the Chief of the Chinese Buccaneers
b) the Queen of the Macao Pirates
c) the Ruler of the Southeast Sea-dogs

How many pirate attacks were made in Indonesian waters in 2004?

a) 34
b) 70
c) 105

From where were £150 million worth of goods stolen in one attack in 1991?

a) the Black Sea
b) the Gulf of Mexico
c) the Mekong River

(answers on page 32)

THE BIGGER THE BETTER

Even huge ships aren't safe from pirates. In 1991, 31 pirate attacks on tankers were reported in Southeast Asia alone.

CHINA CRISIS

Piracy was a huge problem in China in the 1920s. Civil war created hardships for many and some people responded by attacking foreign ships. One pirate leader was Lai Choi San. She made a fortune from stealing valuables and holding people to ransom.

FIGHTING BACK

Ship's captains are warned not to fight pirates if they board. But after the attack is over, naval patrols can be contacted immediately by radio. Radar, helicopters and aircraft are also used to track down the criminals.

HI-TECH HAUL

Pirates aren't hunting for pieces of eight any more. Today, they're out to rob electrical equipment, such as computers and video recorders, cameras and money. The weapons are different, too – flintlock pistols have been replaced by assault rifles and machine guns.

MODERN-DAY PIRATES

If you think pirates belong just in history books, think again! The boats and the treasure may look different, but piracy is still big business even today.

Chinese pirates

NIGHT FRIGHT

Speed is still important to pirates. They wait in power boats in concealed coves ready to zoom out. Many ships today only need a small crew, so it is easy for pirates to overcome them. Attacks are often made in darkness to make the getaway easy, too.

Modern pirates

Index

Quiz answers

- **Page 3** a, a biscuit; b, 40 lashes on the bare back; c, Alexander Selkirk.
- **Page 4** a, Alf; c, 80,000; b, Geena Davis.
- **Page 6** c, warships; a, Sweyn Forkbeard; b, to go on a sea raid.
- **Page 8** c, 60; c, steering the ship; a, the nef.
- **Page 10** b, a dagger; a, frizzen; b, it doesn't rust.
- **Page 12** b, 1724; c, blackjacks; a, to bring good luck.
- **Page 14** b, cousins; b, New Orleans; c, James I.
- **Page 16** a, gold coins; b, they were worth eight reals; b, Gardiner's Island.
- **Page 18** c, Edward Teach; a, The Fancy; c, tea.
- **Page 21** a, North Africa; c, Rock Braziliano; a, Greece.
- **Page 22** b, to pull two ships together; a, a drum; c, spiking the feet of enemies.
- **Page 24** b, the first rope broke; a, keel-hauling; b, 1840.
- **Page 26** c, William Kidd; b, £100; a, to avoid a punishment for poaching.
- **Page 29** b, Gilbert and Sullivan; a, The Black Pig; a, Captain Flint.
- **Page 30** b, the Queen of the Macao Pirates; b, 70; c, the Mekong River.

Acknowledgements

Copyright © 2006 **ticktock** Entertainment Ltd. First published in Great Britain by ticktock Media Ltd., Unit 2, Orchard Business Centre, North Farm Road, Tunbridge Wells, Kent TN2 3XF, Great Britain.

All rights reserved. No part of this publication may be reproduced, stored in a retrieval system, or transmitted in any form or by any means electronic, mechanical, photocopying, recording or otherwise, without prior written permission of the copyright owner.

A CIP catalogue record for this book is available from the British Library.

ISBN 1 86007 955 5 Printed in China.

Picture Credits: t = top, b = bottom, c = centre, l = left, r=right

AKG Photo; 8t, 20/21b, 30/31. Ann Ronan @ Image Select; 1, 22, 26/27. e.t. Archive; 8/9, 18/19. FPG International; 3, 11, 16/17. Image Select; 14. Mary Evans Picture Library; OFC & 2/3, 4, 6, 10/11, 14/15, 22/23, 25r. National Maritime Museum; 20/21t. Rex Features London; 31b. The Kobal Collection; 6/7, 26, 28, 28/29. The Mariners' Museum; 18b, 24, 27.